Presented to

Dear Sheila

from

Pat

On this day

April 2005

With best love.

Sorry to hear you are feeling under the weather.

I hope you're back on top soon.

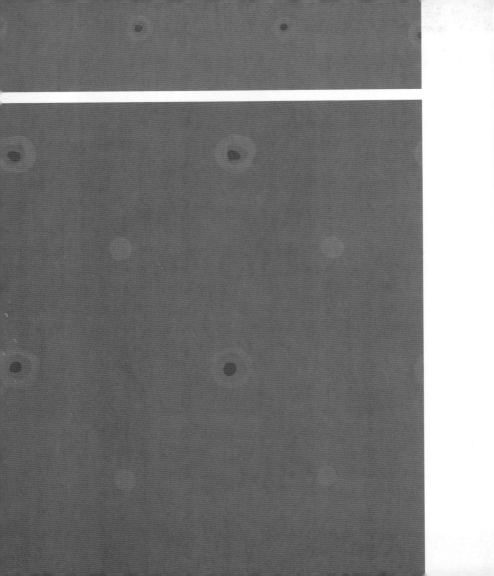

the Bright Side

a unique perspective on feeling under the weather

BY REBECCA GERMANY

ILLUSTRATED BY CINDY REVELL

A DAYMAKER GREETING BOOK

WHEN YOU ARE SICK. . .

*You don't
have to get
out of your
jammies.*

You can

sleep on

the couch.

You don't have to take a shower.

It's nature's way
of telling you to
take a break.
(Your alarm
clock can take a
break too.)

You can catch
up on your
reading of
the great
classics.

You have time to count the specks on your bedroom ceiling.

You can do a
video-watching
marathon.

You can watch

daytime TV.

You're home
to see what
your mailman
looks like.

A dog or cat
makes a good
heating pad.

You have an

excuse for

snoring.

It's okay to want
your mommy.

It's okay
to cry.

You can expect
cards and flowers
you didn't get on
Valentine's Day.

Friends and
family are
willing to
clean up
after you.

You don't
need to fight
rush-hour
traffic.

No one
cares if you
sleep the
day away.

A milkshake is
a main dish.

You tend to lose

extra pounds.

(But. . .you could

gain a few pounds

without guilt.)

Chocolate is
still the
cure-all.

friends

volunteer

to do the

yard work.

You learn the
world really will
keep spinning
without you for a
few days.

You finally have a good excuse to try the motorized scooter at the grocery store.

You can find

comfort in the

Psalms.

You know you

have friends

praying for you.

You become

all the more

grateful for

the times

you are in

good health.

© 2004 by Barbour Publishing, Inc.

ISBN 1-59310-320-4

Illustrated by Cindy Revell.

Designed by Julie Doll.

Published by Barbour Publishing, Inc., P.O. Box 719, Uhrichsville, Ohio 44683,
www.barbourbooks.com

*Our mission is to publish and distribute inspirational products
offering exceptional value and biblical encouragement to the masses.*

Printed in China.
5 4 3 2 1